The Rhyming Sky

The Rhyming Sky

Christopher Hopkins

Clare Songbirds
Publishing House

Clare Songbirds Publishing House Poetry Series
ISBN 978-1-957221-12-0
Clare Songbirds Publishing House
The Rhyming Sky © 2023 Christopher Hopkins

Printed in the United States of America
FIRST EDITION

Clare Songbirds Publishing House
140 Cottage Street
Auburn, New York 13021
www.claresongbirdspub.com

For Mam & Dad

Acknowledgements

I called them wild geese (Oare Marsh) - *The New European, #217.*

The bone blue and the harrier (Oare Marsh) – *Reliquiae, Vol 10 No.1, Corbel Stone Press.*

Blood has been pooling all along (Seasalter) (earlier version) – *Reliquiae, Vol 10 No.1, Corbel Stone Press.*

Dragonfly (Oare) (earlier version) – *Spelt Magazine, issue 6, Summer 2022.*

Contents

Marsh pond (Seasalter)

Eye-dark, fire-dark
its voice, its colour.
The rust-loose pearl
I bless with a pebble.
A trapdoor, a drowning.

One hollow break,
each collar bone O
hurries from this world —
to stillness. A cupped spell.
The rhyming sky.

Its
    fragile
        dark-light.

Walk to last light (Oare Marsh)

The muds are stirring up again.
Jelly spit whites off the knives
of flint breakers, and for the
nettle air – *the sky,*
like a jay's wing.

Thistledown globes on the
May dyke are like an old-
man's milk whiskers,
bobbing jolly for the whistle
to catch just right.

Fill the burst air with dirt-fairy
down. Blow it all inland,
all up town.

... ...

Clouds fist
in the sandstone-wind.
I take the white stone path.
The metal ink in song,
the earth reeds bow.

Hulls, rough as crab skin,
coffee ringed
in salt-dirt,
and reds
are pinkish buoy curves
on the bleached hides
of the rub and rub
from the turned
milk tides,
sea crud
and amen, amen.

The remains of
men. These little work
boats, handless
and love knot tied,
safe home
on dull tide-less,
on the wash of beds —
these little dirt dishes
in soaped water
gone cold.

. . . .

How wind pairs
with wing,

how the high birds spin

4

and gain, writing their
graffitied names over
blue, over
a simple path of
worn warm stone, over
a hip bone
of crushed can,
now tin-aged by years,

and the
summer after
summer
on a carton of
dissolving lungs,
the soft
black crackle
on
cellophane —
when the
rains come.

. . . .

Among our
common yellow,
the flower
in the
blade,
I find a stone island.

A star
voyeur.

A *thing*
forever numb
to the caw of gull
and crab skin white,
to the rise of wind
and kicking sun,

numb
as
the old
exposed
foundation of
the Powder
works.

Man's footprint,
permanent
and lost.

. . . .

In this God
quiet,
in the
never silent
song

listen
to the through-
wind talk.

To a
sun's push
through the
reed's
rub hush,

a leaf-
seed

in boat fall

to its brief legacy
on a marsh pond's
gaze -

a
shiver
on the back of
black waters,

a watching
mirror,

above, the half ghost of
midges
that spirits
the air,

like a lamp-worker,
soul shifter,
in their
copper
magnificence
(crossing themselves).

. . . .

The mill wheel has
sunk below
the shelter
in
the
wicker.

The chatter
of invisible nesting.

The sky is like a
grounded
spell,

colours of the earth
on fire,

movements
on forever-
waters.

. . . .

A drag throat
of seabird,

the way laughter
carries at
dusk.

. . . .

Now, the dust moon.

White on
a viewing
post.

I am with the
frailest
of things

(our world
is forgetting).

. . . .

There is hunger
in the light.

In this shortest

hour the night—
jaws appear.

The dark swifts
of the moth moon
kills. Spirits
above
the field.

The ultra
singing.

. . . .

There are boards in the
diaphragm,
the hour
eating
ashes

and the weight of
a star
heads a rag-a-bone
sea.

The passing of a
late wing.

The air
like a stone
to skin.

The day
cooling,

a change in scent,
like cider rot.

Everything
is watching a
light.

In the oyster
cold
the land is
pulled
into the
beginning

of darkness,

into the ambitions
of night.

Now sound
is the currency,
sound
as
light.

No lullabies
in folding tides,
no world
talking
in her sleep —

now

the night-radio plays,

and sound
is waved,

a busy pitch and
pop of
bird or fox
cough

among algorithms
of
the thorn gauze and
down root dirt,

the insect
rub

on this alter of
night,

while
sleeping
swans fold in
their light —
making bonnet
moons on a
heaven ill.

There
is darkness,

as where the heart
sits in its cage —

with fearing,

as if all of
time gone
is reaching for you.

Rising from earth
with limb & wing,
among the sleep
of roots, out from the
dead crow soil, out
to above the thicket line,

and escapes

into a night sky's
eternal
luxury.

. . . .

A spoil light.
The colour
junk that the
night-lands

throw out

and scatter.
A town-
shaped
light,

some bleb of
promise
off the far
knocking
shore,

(*shopfronts, streetlights
motorway flare*)

so, that the
living
stars
are nothing more
than a tear
shake of
the moon.

. . . .

The night waters
have held up
the bell stars
for so long
they tire into
mirrors —

sick
lights that
fall and shatter,
like
constellations of
obsidian.

They mute and
clef a
wilderness,

a darker
harvest

downwind
from
heaven,
down to
muds of a
river-sea,
in the living sleep

and
are
wonder-less
to the
dark.

....

Gull poem (Whitstable)

Oh, happy gull.
Your call & echo call
are yours alone
grey day angel.

Economy
of song, over the
wrack o' tides in town
centres, papered

silver in your
piss-ghost likeness.
Our little shit swan
of detritus.

Made like winter's
light, you are the
wind-caught, maggot-
gutted
kite. The night sky

drifter, cloud king,
selfish bird of prayer.
You — dull phoenix,
born from
the waste of things.

Early morning coffee at the hide (Oare Marsh)

Sugar cube boats turn to the colour of oceans and sink to the bottom of their china sea — and the night's relief, the dawn's opening saffron and the foreshore's white noise of a turning moon, is released — *the first Golden.* A roof line will soon invade the ache of the rising *light,* while the coffee froth burst comes like the invention of stars. His breath, in the closed cold, his only human company, and like a hopeless wiser heart, it falls into the half Saturn warmth in cupped hands, as he watches a kissing sky.

This world is a gentle mirror.

Do the same waters stir on each estuary tide, or a past and present witchery of waterlines? What myth or math turns the indigo silver? Could this ever be more beautiful? In a collar dark grace of night is how he entered — along a frost path — *as his guiding light,* like stairs into the morning's night (side the shifting of insomnious monsters). And he leaves sun blessed, the incumbent dreamer. A believer that light passes through the heart, conscious of the world's rhapsody and that the winged are in fact immortal. He is learning to see.

Pausing on Hollyhill Road (Dunkirk)

The sally ripple through trough water.
The bright whitening on the green field
in a cloud rhythm of the light and blackbird dart.

The sky is open, but deepening between
heavy black silvers of the passing roll —
of rain cloud and silhouetted cows

and the bright wonder of the monument tree.
Its bearness outstretched, as if frozen pale
touching something unseen, *a world past death,*

and stands as gateway - to some otherness,
some green magic we have evolved to un-see.

I called them wild geese (Oare Marsh)

but they were not,
in the sunstone
dye,
above the ladder web
field, as the fire was
leaving.
A star forced its
white touch upon
the body of
sky, they made
their way,
their
white
bellies
showing.

I called them wild
geese but they
were not,
as the wide eve made
our time so visible by
the blind eye
of the blood-sap
star. A bird's
rushed lullaby
tongue
sung its black
notes, its
white,
sung temperate to
a paper print of a
moon.
Their
easing
skein of
beauty.

I called them wild
geese but they
were not,
when the silence broke
to the language of a
peat-black wing,
like a spirit word,
an unstressed
amen.
They translate
the ore-water
to a gracefulness
of downing,
the spirit
red on the
burning
edge
as the wing
bone caught
the fire.

Nineteen notes written (Oare Marsh)

One – in the kingdom of
sky and green reed
Two – in the kelt sun and
its moon-hood
Three – in the yellow
fall to white
Four – in the shaping of
a marsh-moor flower
Five – in the smallest
melodies on power lines
Six – on our harrow path
Seven – in the poet's
colour
Eight – on the sea wind –
dyke kissing
Nine - in the month of the
bad wound
Ten – a walk in the spark
grit
Eleven – in the
loneliness sun

Twelve – a lug sky
torn clean by the drop
anchor
of peregrine
Thirteen – a feeling for
scattering
Fourteen – always in the
ash pilgrim of a rain
cloud
Fifteen – a year's early
browning
Sixteen – loving and
sadness
Seventeen – devotion
telling in the ill hymn
Eighteen – in each note
wrung
Nineteen – what is learnt
too late of happiness
will always be
the song

Fractal field (Oare Marsh)

The field – a huge spirit of mist.
A sea sky bonded with fractal green.

The crows – black coated, drip on the edge,
globed in wing frowns and oil feathers cold.

The human – figure of a man, through the field's
closed door. *Their* suspicions on his movement
through the blindfolded land.

The ferns – out curl their tender fingers, to feel the stutters
in the universe's affairs, white cloud pricked on hairs.

The sky-thick waters – blessing the walkers sheltering
clothes, with the down seed that travels with him.

The brush – of dandelion quartz, head fulls of
dreaming rainbows. Halo and sun.

The trail – these footprints. The silver of
spent time.

The bone blue and the harrier (Oare Marsh)

The wind doesn't care if you are there,
it'll cut right through you

as you come,
star dour,

to hook your buried heart upon the
wide bone blue

*(a crown of skies to absolve you, a
healing land).*

Its cold will come at you, come thun-
dering down —

to colour the tempest on the dizzying
seed, force a blow through the hollow
reed, flash its knife to colour — the
mud silver of freshwater,

and drown out the crow on the mobbing
wing, put the age in the wrinkled skin
of thorn bark,

the panic in the dart; the black white of
a piper,

the bone blue and the harrier.

The optimist (The way behind The Sportsman, Seasalter)

Sun frost and omega on the wind.
A purple flowering.

Seeing things on the long waters,
between the comber and the
window dark —

I see a lone bird that falters,
reaching for the iron wide —

and as I am caught within their
micro prayer — the bird cuts gentle
the lustre in the dank.

And this thing-itself — hope and
its arrow's wake — becomes wide
as the empire sea.

And I rest, the optimist, with
thoughts of my soul-bird,

its ripple, harboured.

Dragonfly (Church Road, Oare Marsh)

Little gunship
of dragonfly.

Big eyed
electric flyer.

You, in day-
marine

are the
otherworldly;

the gold-green
civilization.

The wild
element.

The spun glint
of your effortlessness,

saved in your
air wing,

is like a window
to morning.

An un-
man

machine.
So ablaze

with life's perfect
strangeness.

Road Winds (Canterbury Rd, Boughton)

Winter simplifies the forest.
Bracken rain turns the clock of seed.
All the ambitious dreaming of summer,
all its green, falling from a whiskey sky,
papering the road winds with ease.
A rebellion of colour on
the wrong side of a rainbow.
The first frost on dissolving leaves.

Don't struggle against the season (Oare Marsh)

The only bitterness allowed is in the bite of wind and samphire, while thorns are the only thing to grow into the wind, so, just be yourself, don't struggle against the season or the rhythm in a sea-wing.

Feel the warmth in the yellow light on the torn paper corpse of a wilderness. Over the eider rags, tipping the bow, in the landscaping wind, on the thickened skins of daisies, where life is stubborn and practical, and tenderness is a seed to wander, in a land of sundials & freshwater —a dreamer's bog-land.

Now let the low sun burn your eyes, and the dying light will resemble any love you care to think about.

The dyke gale (Oare Marsh)

It's like a pulse of ice that
comes across the salt-boon

and I'm no longer
invisible.

Dawn-walking (Oare Marsh)

among the dawn's
silk bowl,
among the air thick
on a cold morning.
Shapes,

buildings,
appearing
part by part

in shadow walls
& window
sleep.

The light
feeling on the
ice braille
for the body of land,
through

pale sills
into
the half-life and sounds, to a
thistle tune

that crooks the
morning
seed —

(*the song of the wintered
blue gulls*)

out,
over the dark wool of
the distant field:
where
a golden
owl
takes
from the ground.

(*tall grasses, earth
white*)

Where the sky
rose
with its
blood.

Blood has been pooling all along (Seasalter)

A hoarse chime, then the grey gulls ghost you —
to walk pebble grasses in the sun's late colours.

Reds, that shape and shadow uneven salts,
and into tin waters come late travellers.

The sky hangs as you imagined love.
A part of you like a spinning coin.

The taken flame. A bird bone moon.
The sea, so bright and dark.

And still the night wants for wildflowers
than the carried lights all torn in rushes —

simple lives and simple wishes,
like petal stars on thorn.

Christopher Hopkins has had poems published in *The Honest Ulsterman*, *Reliquiae Journal*, *The New European*, *Morning Star*, *Spelt Magazine*, *14 Magazine* (Vanguard Readings) and *Rust + Moth* among others. He has three chapbooks with Clare Songbirds Publishing House, New York. Christopher's work has been nominated for the Pushcart prize three times.